Original title:
A Jungle Beneath My Feet

Copyright © 2025 Creative Arts Management OÜ
All rights reserved.

Author: Hugo Fitzgerald
ISBN HARDBACK: 978-1-80581-914-1
ISBN PAPERBACK: 978-1-80581-441-2
ISBN EBOOK: 978-1-80581-914-1

The Symphony of the Ground

Underfoot, the critters dance,
A mouse does salsa, in its pants.
A worm does wiggles, all in sync,
While ants form bands, they'll never shrink.

The earthworms hum a funky beat,
While beetles tap their tiny feet.
A grasshopper joins in with a leap,
And crickets croon before they sleep.

A snail takes stage with a slow glide,
While spiders spin webs, quite the ride.
With each small step, a show unfolds,
Life underground, with laughter bold.

So let us stomp and shake the ground,
For music plays where life is found.
Each shuffle tells a tale so neat,
In this delightful, funny feat.

Beneath the Canopy of Dreams

The roots are gossiping, oh my!
They twist and turn, say, 'Do not fly!'
The ferns have secrets, oh how they sigh,
While mushrooms giggle, beneath the sky.

The ants are crafting their own parade,
With tiny flags, in line they wade.
A lizard mocks them with a grin,
As beetles spin tales of old within.

A toad croaks jokes, a ribbit or two,
While dandelions bloom with morning dew.
The sunbeams chuckle, bright and keen,
As they dance on leaves, a playful scene.

So let us wander where laughter grows,
Among the roots where joy bestows.
In this merry patch, we'll find a seat,
And share our dreams, all warm and sweet.

The Tapestry of Life Below

In the soil, critters scurry,
Fungus dances, never in a hurry.
Worms throw a disco in the earth,
Celebrating their underground birth.

Beneath the bark, a party grows,
Ants do the conga, as everyone knows.
With beetles grooving to a silent beat,
The laughter rises from every seat.

Currents of Color in the Dark

Frogs wear tiaras, croaking a tune,
Fireflies twinkle like stars in June.
Mice in sunglasses, ready to dance,
Under moonlight, they'll take a chance.

Rats with paintbrushes splash the night,
Creating murals by the soft moonlight.
Unseen artists, oh such a show,
In this vibrant land that we'll never know.

Surprises Waiting in the Undergrowth

Beneath the leaves, a comedy waits,
A hedgehog's hat and three tiny plates.
Squirrels gossip about the new trend,
That acorns are just a means to an end.

A shy snail prepares for the grand ball,
With sequined shell, he stands proud and tall.
While rabbits debate the best kind of hat,
Arguing styles, oh imagine that!

Where the Wild Things Lurk

A raccoon in pajamas, sneaking a snack,
Doughnuts hidden in a makeshift pack.
They giggle and shuffle in quiet delight,
As mischief unfolds deep into the night.

Geckos holding a fashion parade,
Strutting their colors, magnificent shade.
While frogs play poker, bets made with flies,
Under the stars, beneath twinkling skies.

Journeying Through a Living Tapestry

In a forest thick with chatter,
Where every twig seems a guy,
I stumbled on a dancing rat,
Wearing leaves as his bow tie.

The ferns are laughing at my shoes,
They squeak and squawk with glee,
As I trip and twirl like a fool,
In this wacky jamboree.

Mushrooms bounce like little clowns,
Casting jokes from the shade,
A beetle rolls a tiny cart,
Of nachos he'd just made.

Nature's jesters keep me guessing,
With a twist and a twirl,
Who knew that ground could be so grand,
In this tangled up world?

Vines that Cradle the Ground

Vines wiggle and they giggle,
   Embracing roots below,
They've formed a jungle dance floor,
   With swing moves all aglow.

I tried to join their merry ball,
   But tangled up my knees,
Now I'm twirling with the grasses,
   Swaying with the breeze.

The crickets sing their cheeky songs,
   While caterpillars slide,
And I, a mere clumsy dancer,
   Keep slipping with my pride.

In this twisty, turning waltz,
   Each step's a laughing spree,
With vines that cradle all the ground,
   Dancing wild and free!

Beneath the Bark and Leaf

A chipmunk in a fedora struts,
Claiming all the land,
While squirrels hold a nut debate,
With a judge that's pretty grand.

The raccoons wear their masks so sly,
They plot a midnight feast,
As I try to sneak a peek,
But trip on roots, at least!

Underneath the leafy shade,
Where laughter's quite the speech,
The shadows play their silly games,
For this is life's rich peach.

With bark so thick and leaves a-sway,
The flora's full of glee,
I'm just a guest in this mad land,
Where nature laughs with me!

When Shadows Paint the Undergrowth

In shadows deep, where tall grass sways,
   I spotted a dancing toad,
  He croaks out tunes of silly ways,
    As if he's on the road.

A family of ants in bright hard hats,
  March on with a grand parade,
  While butterflies audition plays,
 In the leaf of fate they've made.

The playful sun, it winks just right,
  As lizards strike a pose,
 I joined the party on a whim,
  But hey, I can't disclose!

With shadows painting every scene,
 The undergrowth takes flight,
 In this comical chaos of life,
  Everything feels just right!

The Veiled Kingdom Below

In the grass, a brigade of ants,
Marching as if they had big plans.
Their tiny hats, oh what a sight,
Holding meetings 'til the moon's light.

A worm attempts a tango dance,
With a snail who won't take a chance.
Laughing leaves join in the tease,
Whispering secrets in the breeze.

Harmony in the Wild

A frog croaks opera, quite absurd,
While crickets play the bass unheard.
The parakeets laugh from above,
And every branch is filled with love.

A raccoon steals my sandwich, grins,
While squirrels plan their acorn wins.
Together they form a wacky band,
In the wild, always unplanned.

The Lattice of Existence

Under leaves, a disco scene,
Where plants and bugs get rather keen.
A caterpillar spins in glee,
While a snail says, 'Not for me!'

Spider webs catch sunlight's spark,
And fireflies dance into the dark.
A mongoose wears a feathered hat,
Declaring, 'I am styling, that's that!'

Palpable Paradox

A tree that's tall but feels so small,
With fruits that giggle, springing a brawl.
A mushroom's sigh, like whispered jokes,
Elicits laughter from surrounding folks.

Hippos hide behind a curtain of vines,
Playing peek-a-boo, plotting their signs.
In this strange realm, where oddities greet,
Life's quirks are a bizarre treat!

Beneath the Surface

In the soil, a party's begun,
Worms wear hats, it's all in fun.
Beetles bust a synchronized dance,
While ants in tuxedos prance.

Roots are networking, making deals,
Photosynthesis—they're the real deals.
Grasshoppers crack jokes, oh what a sight,
While critters lounge 'neath the moonlight.

Life Thrives

Tiny frogs wear tiny crowns,
Hopping 'round in leafy towns.
Chirping crickets start to play,
While moths come out for the cabaret.

Ladybugs are fashion stars,
Chatting under glowworm bars.
Flowers giggle in the breeze,
With nectar served like expert teas.

Footfalls on Fertile Ground

Every step on this soft bed,
Causes laughter, not much dread.
Squirrels throwing acorn pies,
While a toad winks with bulging eyes.

A sloth croons a slow, sweet song,
Takes its time, can't get it wrong.
Raccoons in masks on scavenger hunts,
Find treasures amidst the roots and brunts.

Where Silence Holds Court

In the quiet, laughter breeds,
Mice gather round to share their leads.
A chameleon tells silly tales,
Of colorful queens and their flashy gales.

Mushrooms giggle in their spots,
While sleepy snakes twist up in knots.
In whispers, secrets long cosigned,
By leaves that rustle, soft and kind.

Rustlings in the Thickets

Thickets rustle, giggles bloom,
As critters break out from the gloom.
Rabbits toss their fluffy hats,
In a maze of playful spats.

A clever tortoise plans a race,
Slow and steady sets the pace.
All rejoice in the hidden cheer,
Nature's hilarity brings us near.

Echoes of the Untraveled Trail

In the grass, a cricket sings,
While ants parade with tiny wings.
A squirrel sneezes, a branch may sway,
As leaves whisper secrets of the day.

Oh, what mischief lies below,
A mouse slips by, just to say hello!
The ground's alive with giggles and grunts,
While worms throw parties with their funky bunts.

The Life Beneath Our Steps

When I stomp loud, the beetles flee,
They think my shoes are a sight to see!
The earthworms wiggle, plot their escape,
While snails curl up—oh, what a shape!

A toad in the mud gives me the eye,
As if to say, 'What a clumsy guy!'
With every step, the drama unfolds,
In this realm of critters, stories untold.

A Chorus of the Unseen

Footprints danced in the morning dew,
Echoes of tiny creatures too!
A grasshopper plays a tiny tune,
While mushrooms giggle beneath the moon.

Each stride I take, a laugh or squeak,
The shadows whisper, they're far from meek.
With each little hop and tiny creep,
The world beneath warms softly, no need for sleep.

Tales of the Ground We Walk

Beneath my toes, a party's begun,
With critters and fungi, oh what fun!
A lizard darts—oh, what a sight,
As beetles disco under the light.

The roots below weave stories old,
Of sunlit days and secrets bold.
With giggles and squawks, the underworld thrives,
Each step I take, it dances and dives.

The Enchantment of Hidden Realms

In the brush, a critter dances,
With tiny shoes and silly prances.
He lifts a leaf, a crown of glory,
In this green world, it's quite a story.

The ants are marching, quite a parade,
In their tiny suits, they've got it made.
They tip their hats, then dive for snacks,
Living large while we sit back.

A frog in shades lounges on a toad,
Sipping dew on the humor road.
He croaks a tune, a croaky song,
In this wild realm, nothing feels wrong.

Lizards gossip, tails a-flap,
Swapping tales on a mossy map.
With every step, I tread with glee,
In this funny realm, I'm wild and free.

Guardians of the Verdant Depths

Two squirrels, rascals, plan their schemes,
Hiding acorns in our wild dreams.
With tiny capes, they save the day,
In the great outdoors, they dance and play.

A parrot squawks, a colorful sage,
Reads the news, then starts a stage.
With beaks of wisdom, they squawk and cheer,
Making forest life a laugh-filled sphere.

Underneath a bramble, a hedgehog snores,
Dreaming of cheese and far-off shores.
Awake, he tumbles, a ball of spikes,
Rolling 'round, delighting hikes.

A chameleon changes, just for fun,
Becoming furniture under the sun.
When you look away, he takes a peek,
Sprinkles giggles among the bleak.

Marvels Where No Eyes Wander

A snail with flair slides down the trail,
Wearing a shell that's quite the tale.
He stops for tea, invites a bug,
Matters of life, they each give a shrug.

A butterfly flutters in goofy loops,
Tripping on nectar with all the troops.
He chats with blooms, a floral roast,
In this wild place, he's the host with the most.

The beetles rumble, a rock band crew,
Jamming to beats in the morning dew.
With antennae waving, they play their riffs,
In the concert of life, they're the best gifts.

A turtle grins, slow but wise,
Winks at clouds that drift by the skies.
In this vast world that's fun and bright,
He's off on the journey of pure delight.

A Siesta of Shadows and Light

Under leafy umbrellas, a sloth hangs tight,
Dreaming of tacos, oh, what a sight!
With a sleepy grin, he waves his paw,
In this chill zone, spirits never flaw.

A raccoon dines, munching on chips,
In moonlight's glow, he does funny flips.
"What's for dessert?" he looks to the stars,
"Maybe some cake from Venus or Mars!"

A spider spins webs, quite the designer,
Catching laughs, the world's top liner.
With each tangle, he sways and hums,
In this webbed wonder, feel the fun drums.

A firefly winks, a disco light,
Guiding the night in sequins bright.
We shuffle and sway under twinkling beams,
In shadows and light, we dance our dreams.

When Footfalls Conceal Adventures

Every step I take is met
By rustling leaves and branches wet.
I trip on roots like good ol' friends,
Are they helping me or making amends?

Unseen creatures peek and stare,
Echoes of laughter fill the air.
I name the bugs and name their roles,
Crickets are jesters, the ladybugs, souls.

With my shoes as an all-terrain boat,
Each stomp's an adventure, a funny note.
I leap like a frog, but fall like a stone,
This trek through green, I'm never alone.

A squirrel chuckles from a high tree,
As I dance 'round puddles, wild and free.
The world below springs tales so neat,
Who knew footfalls led to such a treat?

The Color of What Lies Below

Oh, where's the path, is it here or there?
Green things bounce, with snacks to share.
I spotted blue — is that a shoe?
Nope, just a berry, looking quite new.

With an army of ants all marching in line,
They sent me a message, 'You'll be just fine.'
I ask if they'd join me for tea one day,
But they scramble away, come what may.

Then there's a worm doing the twist,
In a disco party that I merely missed.
A rainbow of colors all danced 'neath my toes,
Tiny delights in the land where plants grow.

As I laugh at the mess of dirt on my shoe,
The vibrant earth whispers, 'Join the crew!'
Adventure is waiting with a quirky display,
My feet lead the way while the world goes 'Hooray!'

The Voice of the Hidden World

Hear that giggle? What could it be?
It's just the grass, whispering to me.
The earth is singing, a cheeky tune,
While mushrooms nodding, want to join soon.

A pebble quips, 'I've seen it all!'
As I stumble upon a tree so tall.
Each root and twig has a secret to share,
And the shadows just wink as I start to stare.

The leaves exchange gossip, tittering light,
While shadows race around, playing at night.
With every crunch, a joke might unfold,
In this banquet of laughter, I'm perfectly bold.

So when I ramble down this funny road,
I'll listen close to the giggles bestowed.
In this orchestra of sights, sound and cheer,
Every footstep's a song, loud and clear!

In the Embrace of Unseen Roots

Tangled ties beneath the floor,
A comedy act of roots galore.
They tickle toes and startle my shoes,
Offering laughter, with nothing to lose.

With each cautious step, I dance and prance,
Caught in the sway of my own silly chance.
Who knew below the world so stout,
Was a merry troupe just waiting to shout?

I fumble and tumble, not quite a star,
Yet the buried dancers cheer, 'You'll go far!'
Each branch takes a bow while I trip and sway,
In this world underground, I find my way.

As the ground giggles, I blush and beam,
A world so absurd, it's part of the dream.
So here's to the roots, in fun and in jest,
For in their embrace, I've truly been blessed!

Veils of Life Underground

In the depths where critters creep,
A meeting where the ants all leap,
Beneath the soil, they hold a ball,
With tiny hats, they dance and sprawl.

Worms wear ties, oh what a sight,
They wiggle and twirl with sheer delight,
The moles, in shades, adjust their glasses,
As fireflies flash in grassy masses.

A beetle DJ spins the tunes,
While spiders serve up sticky looms,
They toss confetti made of leaves,
Creating tales that none believes.

When I ponder their wild jest,
I laugh and think, I'm truly blessed,
For under the ground, life's a spree,
More fun than I could ever see!

Mapping the Unseen

Beneath my feet, with footloose flair,
Are paths where neither man nor bear,
Have placed a foot to leave a trace,
In hidden realms, a wily race.

A troupe of toads plays hopscotch there,
While snails race with a slower glare,
Each rock a weathered totem pole,
With soggy maps of soil's control.

The roots below have secret plans,
They form alliances with ants and cans,
They giggle jokes in earthy tones,
These crafty couriers on their stones.

With laughter echoing in my mind,
I wonder what treasures I might find,
As life beneath spins a merry dance,
In a world where shadows take a chance.

Tendrils of Connection

Intertwined in earthy bliss,
Vines whisper secrets we might miss,
They giggle gently with each sway,
As I walk on, they seem to play.

Roots exchange gossip, oh so loud,
The mushrooms chuckle, standing proud,
They share tall tales of sneaky bugs,
That scurry past in hurried shrugs.

Fun-loving ferns flail in the breeze,
While thorns conspire to bring you to knees,
The ground beneath, a chatty crew,
With every step, they laugh anew.

In tangled hugs they weave their fate,
I can't help but join their silly state,
For life below is quite the show,
In this quirky world where funny things grow.

The Forgotten Symphony

In the earth, a tickle thrives,
Composed by ants as life contrives,
A melody of shuffles, hums,
With rhythm marked by bugger drums.

The beetles tune their shiny shells,
And firefly lights cast wondrous spells,
Each rustle writes a new refrain,
As nature joins in this sweet gain.

Crickets chirp in playful rows,
While nearby roots engage in prose,
They shake their leaves and pull a note,
A harmony on which to float.

I stand above, they play the score,
In laughter's dance, I find much more,
For underground, a symphony,
Creating joy that's wild and free!

Breath of the Untamed

I tripped on vines, oh what a sight,
A lizard laughed, just took flight.
The monkeys giggle in the trees,
While I step softly, trying to freeze.

A frog in shorts, how very bold,
Telling stories never told.
With each squish and each slide,
I find myself in a comical ride.

The leaves are whispering silly tunes,
While squirrels dance beneath the moons.
I laugh, I slip, I spin around,
In this wild world, pure joy is found.

A parrot squawked, "You're in my space!"
I bowed my head, still holding grace.
Nature's antics, a comedic show,
With every step, where will I go?

The Pulse of the Underworld

Down below, where roots entwine,
I found a beetle sipping wine.
The worms held parties every night,
While ants dressed up to take flight.

A snail wore shades, oh what a scene,
Claiming the title of jungle queen.
The earthworms boogie, a wiggly cheer,
I chuckle softly, they must have no fear.

Beneath the path, the secrets hum,
While creatures shuffle, oh what fun!
I tried to dance but tripped instead,
And landed softly, it's all in my head.

In the shadows, whispers raced,
A raccoon winked, oh how I faced!
With every thump and cheerful beat,
This buzzing world, I cannot beat.

Tangles of Green and Gold

A vine I thought might let me swing,
Turned out to be a slothish king.
With fuzzy feet and sleepy eyes,
He looked at me, oh my, surprise!

The sunlight giggled, danced with flair,
While I was tangled up in hair.
The flowers chuckled, colors bright,
As I fumbled left and then took flight.

A squirrel tossed acorns just for fun,
"Catch me if you can!" it exclaimed, run!
I ran and slipped, an acorn hit,
And suddenly I did a split.

The earth was laughing, oh what a show,
While muddy paws said, "Just go with the flow!"
With every stomp and every fall,
Nature reveals the best of all.

Muffled Songs of the Foliage

The leaves would hum a silly tune,
As I tried to dance beneath the moon.
A raccoon crooned a catchy song,
While I bobbed along, what could go wrong?

The grumpy plants seemed quite absurd,
Grumbling softly, sharing a word.
My toe got stuck in a muddy patch,
I laughed so hard, it was quite the catch.

A squirrel hosted a feast of nuts,
I joined the circle, but fell on my guts.
The dandelions perked up their head,
Singing loudly, "Come join!" they said.

With each adventure, the humor flows,
Amidst the shrubs, where silliness grows.
In every step, be ready for fun,
In this shady place, we've only begun.

An Exploration of Earthly Wonders

Under my shoes, a world to explore,
Tiny creatures having a score.
Worms with their squiggles take delight,
As ants march on, like soldiers in flight.

Leaves whisper secrets to soil so grand,
Tickling toes on this earthy sand.
Roots play tag, stretching all about,
While crickets debate if they should shout!

Every step, a dance, oh what a find!
With each little poke, a giggle unwind.
I stumble on mushrooms, those funny hats,
Trying to be careful 'round all the fats!

My shoes are now stained with dirt and cheer,
As nature chuckles right in my ear.
With each little hop, a comical twirl,
This hidden realm makes my heart unfurl.

The Murmuring Melodies of the Floor

With each step I take, the ground does hum,
A chorus of critters playing their drum.
The beetles are buzzing a catchy tune,
While snails slide in rhythm beneath the moon.

Grasshoppers leap in a joyous jig,
Twirling around like they've had a big swig!
Squirrels complain with a twitch of their tail,
As I trip on roots, oh what a grand fail!

Every pebble beneath offers a jest,
As I slip and slide; what a wild quest!
Nature's own band in this lively show,
Reminds me that laughter is best to sow!

Through mud and through moss, the fun never ends,
In this comical place where the gnome pretends.
Step lightly my friend, let your spirit soar,
For the melodies await on this earthen floor.

Phantoms of the Vegetative Realm

With each stride I take, I'm not all alone,
Ghosts of the weeds pull me back to their zone.
These phantom plants giggle while I try to flee,
Sprouting forth stems that tickle my knee.

Mushroom men dancing in shades of green,
Waving their caps in a comical scene.
The flowers throw shade with their flamboyant flair,
While roots play peekaboo, like they just don't care!

A glance at the ferns waves a friendly hello,
As thorns start a poke – a game to bestow!
These spirited vines whisper jokes so sly,
As I laugh with the leaves, 'Oh my, oh my!'

Each step is a laugh on this path that's alive,
Among shadows and giggles, I jump and I dive.
In a world of green phantoms that leap and spin,
The tales of the soil make me chuckle within.

The Cradle of Nature's Dreams

Beneath my feet, a slumbering maze,
Where earthworms are dreaming in wriggly ways.
The roots hold a riddle, a tale of delight,
While beetles gather round for a chat late at night.

Flowers snooze gently, their petals all curled,
As shadows dance softly in this sleepy world.
Grass blades become pillows for weary bugs,
Sharing tales of the dew and the morning hugs.

The murmurs of nature create quite a scene,
With giggles and whispers from well-napped green.
I pass by the daisies, their heads bobbing low,
Laughing at hiccups of frogs in a row.

So here I will roam, with a chuckle and glee,
In the cradle of dreams where all critters flee.
Step lightly, dear friend, through this whimsical floor,
For here lies the power of laughter galore.

Footsteps on a Mysterious Path

I tread on tangles, wild and free,
Where vines are laughing, just like me.
Each step's a giggle, each twist a cheer,
As branches tease and tug my ear.

A squirrel dances, thinks he's suave,
While puddles wobble, like a wave.
With every stomp, the ferns reply,
I wonder if the ferns can fly?

My shoes are muddy, oh what a sight!
Did I just hear a toad recite?
The path's a riddle, with jokes to share,
With every turn, more antics flare!

But should I shout, or should I hide?
The shadows hold a giggling tide.
So on I march, through giggles and glee,
In this bizarre land, it's just for me!

Roots that Embrace the Unknown

Beneath my feet, the roots engage,
They wiggle, twist, uncage the sage.
A dance of folly, underground's jest,
Where rubbery vines know how to rest.

With every step, they grip and sigh,
As if to ask, 'Hey! Want to fly?'
I laugh and stumble, while they entwine,
Is this a trick? Oh! What divine!

A root tickles my shoe and squeaks,
While worms gossip in hushed, sly peeks.
The soil is rich with stories old,
Of cozy burrows and treasures told.

So here I stand, a giggling fool,
On this vibrant, living stool.
The roots begin their rhythmic beat,
In nature's laugh, I find my seat!

The Hidden Symphony of Green

In the emerald depths, secrets play,
The leaves burst into a jazzy sway.
A whistle from a vine, a croak from below,
Nature's orchestra puts on a show!

Branches tap dance on the soft breeze,
Moss hums along, as chill creeps with ease.
Each rustle a note, each critter a tune,
The daisies bloom in time with the moon.

I can hear a beetle soloing loud,
While ants breakdance, so very proud.
The greenery chuckles, what a parade,
The funny rhythm is never delayed!

So join this bash, where laughter rings,
In a symphony played by tiny things.
With each gentle sway, I find sweet delight,
In this hidden concert, every night!

Sounds of Life Beneath the Soil

Under my soles, a ruckus thrives,
A chorus of critters, all in hives.
The worms are whispering, secrets bold,
And ants are bickering over gold.

Rooted in laughter, their chatter erupts,
While moles hum tunes from cozy cups.
"Keep it down!" I shout, in jest and cheer,
But they giggle back, "We're not here to fear!"

Oh, to hear them bicker, it's quite a thrill,
Life hidden below, with raucous skill.
They plot their journeys under the ground,
With a rhythm of chaos, quite profound.

So let me dance on the verdant above,
While below, they plot, like mischievous love.
I grin for the ruckus, the fun meets the soil,
For beneath me lies life in constant toil!

Living with the Undergrowth

Tiny critters dance around,
In this leafy, green playground.
I trip on roots while trying to flee,
From squirrels claiming all my tea.

Mushrooms sprout without a care,
Waving wands with an open air.
"Hey, don't eat me!" they plead from below,
Fine dining in the mud, what a show!

Vines tickle toes like playful mice,
Each step a challenge, oh so nice.
I laugh as they pull me down to crawl,
This green carpet's ready for a brawl!

But oh, the fun of being ensnared,
In a world where nothing's quite prepared.
With every slip and slide and laugh,
I find adventure in nature's path.

Interludes of the Forest Floor

Footsteps crunch on crunchy leaves,
In a land where mischief weaves.
A slug sidles, slow and grand,
While a sneaky ant steals my planned.

Rabbits munch on bits of grass,
As squirrels wave like classless sass.
"Excuse me, folks!" I shout with glee,
You've got the party, shelter me!

With each plop and plunk I go,
Even spiders steal the show.
Ensnared in webs of giggling vines,
My own dance party, and look—no signs!

Springy moss tickles my feet,
And I stumble on this uneven seat.
Each time I laugh, I make friends anew,
With every bounce, there's much to pursue!

Whispers of the Underbrush

The underbrush has secrets to share,
With giggles lost in scented air.
Glimmering eyes under leaves of green,
A party's brewing, if you know what I mean.

A frog croaks in a karaoke show,
While toads take front row, stealing the glow.
"Join us, friend!" they ribbit with style,
So I sway in rhythm, all the while.

Beetles bumble, they cheerfully clank,
In an orchestra no one would thank.
I try to dance, but oh, what a sight,
As I trip on roots under the moonlight.

Laughter echoes through hidden nooks,
In this wild world, in shady books.
Where every leaf hides a tale to unfurl,
And life's a laugh in this vibrant whirl.

Secrets Buried in Earth

Beneath the soil, a kingdom thrives,
With worms and grubs and playful jives.
The ground's alive with secrets untold,
In the bustling world of the brave and bold.

Fungi giggle, hiding their heads,
While ants parade in conga threads.
"Who invited you?" they question with glee,
As I join their dance, full of esprit.

Wandering roots, they twist and twine,
Sprouting odd dreams, all so divine.
Stumbling over treasures concealed,\nI find my laughter in what is revealed.

From shadows deep where critters creep,
To chirps and rustles that never sleep.
With each step through muck and dirt I find,
That joy and chaos are so entwined.

Breaths of Life from Below

Beneath the ground, a giggle swells,
Grumpy worms in their cozy shells.
A tickle twist where critters play,
As roots do dance in a silly sway.

Mice munch seeds with a dance so neat,
While ants are running their tiny fleet.
A chorus loud from the earth's embrace,
Makes the soil chuckle, a lively space.

The beetles march in a wobbly line,
Whispering jokes, feeling just fine.
A mushroom hat on a toad's small head,
Stories bubble up from the damp and dead.

With every step, a giggle churns,
In every nook, the mischief burns.
So when I tread on this squishy ground,
I hear the laughter, oh so profound.

The Lullaby of Unseen Creatures

Underneath the leafy spread,
Sing lullabies, the ground is wed.
Crickets chirp a bedtime tune,
While fireflies blink like stars at noon.

Moles dive deep in a silent race,
With squashy cheeks and a playful face.
A symphony of snickers arise,
From creatures hidden beneath the skies.

Twirling roots with a ticklish tease,
Whisper secrets to the sneezes of bees.
The soil hums with a playful sound,
As shadows dance on the sumpy ground.

Close your eyes, let laughter soar,
In this haven, there's always more.
The world below, a merry sight,
Where giggles float like stars at night.

Tales Told by the Whispering Roots

Roots weave tales in a jolly light,
Gossiping ferns, what a delight!
Sassy squirrels share their news,
While mushrooms spread stories, no time to snooze.

The ground rumbles with a belly laugh,
As hedgehogs plot their silly craft.
With mischief brewing among the grass,
Even the stones clink and sass.

A tapestry rich, with laughter spun,
Ants tiptoe, their cake is done.
Jubilant whispers float around,
Where each little sprout wears a crown.

Swaying night blooms hum a ditty,
Winking cheekily, how very witty!
These roots hold secrets; so much to tell,
In this lively kingdom where all creatures dwell.

Footprints on Nature's Canvas

Across the patch where I strut and prance,
Hilarious squawks set the mood for dance.
A trail of prints in the muddy spree,
While giggling flowers sway with glee.

Each step I take is a joke retold,
The petals laugh, their colors bold.
A snail wears glasses; oh, what a sight,
Reciting poems in the soft moonlight.

Footprints weave through the forest cheer,
Mice chuckle softly, drawing near.
A splatter of mud is a master stroke,
Nature's canvas, a laughing folk.

The bright-eyed sprites peek out to play,
As my shadow dances the funny way.
In every stride, a joy unfolds,
While nature's art, a tale retold.

Nature's Cryptic Relics

Amidst the leaves, a snail took flight,
Claiming he's a rocket blight.
He zoomed past ants, who cheered with glee,
"Next up: our trip to the big oak tree!"

A worm named Wally wore a hat,
Said, "I'm dapper—not just a flat!"
He wobbled proudly, showed his flair,
But lost it all in a muddy square.

A lonely toad croaked a joke,
"I'm not a prince—I'm just a bloke!"
The flies all laughed, they rolled in mirth,
For royalty here had little worth.

So come and hear the forest speak,
Where critters dance and laughter's peak.
Nature's quirk's a lively feat,
In realms where oddities enjoy their seat.

In the Shadow of Giants

Beneath a tree as wide as a car,
A squirrel claimed he was a star.
"Heard my acorn's now famous on vine,
Next week's talk show? I'll eat fine!"

A beetle strutted, chest held high,
"Watch me shine, I'm the apple pie!"
But tripped on roots, fell with a thud,
"Next time, I'll just roll in the mud!"

The flowers giggled with colors bright,
"Look at those critters—what a sight!"
They swayed with laughter, petals alight,
Nature's comedy—such pure delight!

In shadows grand, where big ones reign,
Tiny tales bring joy, not pain.
Join in this fun, let spirits roam,
The forest floor feels just like home.

Beneath the Canopy's Embrace

A lizard danced with mismatched shoes,
Twirled in circles, shared his blues.
"Do the wiggle, join my spree,
But please don't step on Mr. Bee!"

The parrot squawked, "Hey, what's the news?"
"Just our insects with funny views!
They tell me jokes while munching leaves,
In this place, you just believe!"

A fox with flair had painted fur,
Wore shades of green, oh what a stir!
"Am I a tree or just a tease?
Guess I'm the life of this old breeze!"

So under skies with leaves above,
Life is quirky, it's filled with love.
Join the party, jump in the fun,
In nature's realm, we're all as one.

Life's Lair Awaits

In a burrow deep, a rabbit sprawls,
"Good luck getting up from these walls!"
Chubby friends giggle, roll around,
"I bet digging's just underground!"

A mulberry bush held a tea so sweet,
Sipping slowly, critters come to greet.
"Do tell the tales of your little snares,
And who lost their lunch in the wild lairs!"

The raccoon regaled with shiny stuff,
"I found a spoon—the world's gone tough!
Join our banquet, make a toast,
To far-off dreams, we love the most!"

So gather round, let laughter ring,
In hidden spots, where joys take wing.
Life's little lairs are joy-filled chimes,
Where each burrow beats with silly rhymes.

Nature's Secret Archive

In the thicket where the ants play,
Squirrels throw acorns like they're on display.
A snail takes a selfie, a twig as a prop,
While grasshoppers dance, they just can't stop.

Bees argue loudly about who's the best,
While flowers gossip, they put them to the test.
A frog croaks jokes, making crickets roll,
In this vibrant library, nature's on a stroll.

Mushrooms wear hats, oh what a sight,
While the toadstools giggle throughout the night.
The wind tells tales as it rustles the trees,
Nature's humor blows by, with the greatest of ease.

The roots are comedians, with scenes unplanned,
Giving it all in this green wonderland.
With each step I take, I hear laughter's tune,
In the secret archive beneath the moon.

Guardians of the Leafy Realm

Mice in armor guard their cheese,
While dandelions sway and tease the breeze.
A parrot in shades has style so slick,
With wise old trees, that share a quick trick.

The butterflies plot a bright parade,
While frogs form bands, unafraid.
Lizards do yoga beside a sunbeam,
In the leafy realm, there's always a dream.

Raccoons wear masks to evade the law,
Rolling in leaves, they're the funniest flaw.
Twirling and spinning, a dance so neat,
In this vibrant realm, they never face defeat.

With laughter and whimsy, each creature cheers,
Guardians of nature, bringing us to tears.
In the realm of the green, where silliness blooms,
Every corner's alive with giggles and zooms.

Whispers that Call to Wanderers

Leaves murmur secrets when the sun drops low,
Inviting the wanderers, with tales in tow.
A creature in pajamas peeks from a bush,
While the night critters giggle, giving a push.

Fireflies flicker, play hide and seek,
As the owls hoot hilariously unique.
A raccoon pops confetti from a random stash,
While the silver moon dances in a dazzling flash.

Shadowy figures prance in the gloom,
Carrying jokes that make flowers bloom.
Roots chuckle beneath, with mirth in their grip,
Wanderers chuckle at each unexpected trip.

The whispers entangle in a merry spree,
Calling out laughter, wild and free.
In the night's embrace, where mischief unspools,
Nature's jesters remind us, we're all just fools.

Stories Woven in Roots

Beneath the earth, the stories spin,
With roots like threads, where giggles begin.
A gopher's got tales that would make you grin,
Of treasure hunts where no one could win.

Lively mushrooms trade tales of the day,
While worms twist lines in a humorous way.
An earthworm says, "Hey, I'm the best at hide!"
While a beetle exclaims he's world-famous, worldwide.

The squirrels keep laughing, their antics on cue,
In their fuzzy jackets—they think they are cool.
A hedgehog rolls past, but forgot his hat,
And the laughter erupts at this ridiculous spat.

Amidst tiny giggles and stories of yore,
Life beneath the soil is never a bore.
So tiptoe with grace, as you wander and look,
In this tangled tale, you'll love every nook.

Shadows Dancing in the Understory

In the thicket, shadows glide,
Mice in sneakers, what a ride!
Lizards laughing, playing tricks,
Chasing after fallen sticks.

Frogs perform a croaky show,
To the beat of nature's flow.
A squirrel juggles nuts in air,
While birds gossip without a care.

Worms wear hats, think they look grand,
Dancing like they own the land.
Toadstools wobble, full of cheer,
Nature's circus, what a sphere!

In this world where vines entwine,
Life's a party, oh so fine.
So next time you stop to see,
Join their dance, and you'll agree!

Veins of Nature's Breath

Roots are tickling underground,
Sneaky squirrels gather 'round.
Mossy carpets, soft and green,
In this realm, all's a routine.

Insects marching, forming lines,
Follow the breadcrumbs like some signs.
A beetle drops his lunch, it's true,
And all the bugs laugh, 'A stew!'

Puddles giggle, splashing around,
While ants hold meetings, quite profound.
The breeze whispers jokes to the trees,
With branches swaying, dancing with ease.

Beneath the earth, fun takes root,
Nature's laughter, oh, so cute.
So crouch a bit and join the fun,
Where sunlight fades and shadows run!

Echoes from the Forest Floor

Crickets chirp a goofy tune,
While mushrooms dance beneath the moon.
Acorns tumble, rolling wide,
While sleepy owls try to hide.

Silly splashes, frogs at play,
Sneakered raccoons on parade today.
Leaves are whispering secret jokes,
As playful winds tease the oaks.

Squirrels wear their autumn best,
Flying down on nature's quest.
Every rustle, giggle, cheer,
The laughter echoes, oh so clear.

In this wildness, life does sway,
With every twist in a funny way.
So listen close, and you might hear,
The forest's chuckles far and near!

Beneath Canopies of Dreams

Under leaves, the critters plot,
Bumbling beetles, dancing hot.
A snail slips on a juicy grape,
Hiccups cause an awkward shape.

The sun peeks through a leafy hat,
A chubby chipmunk sings, 'What's that?'
Wiggly worms in bowties twirl,
In this space, the laughter unfurl.

Frantic flowers, they all prance,
Bright colors in a joyful dance.
A butterfly's dressed to delight,
With sparkly wings that catch the light.

Through this maze of fun and glee,
Nature's laughter sets us free.
So pirouette, let spirits soar,
In playful rhythm, dance some more!

Whispers of the Earth Below

The ground giggles softly at my toes,
Worms having parties, nobody knows.
Dancing beetles with their shiny shells,
Whispering secrets of their little spells.

Ants march by, all dressed in black,
They look so serious, never off track.
I wave to a bug, it winks and flies,
Maybe it's a spy in a small disguise.

Mushrooms sprout, a funky crew,
Inviting me to join in their brew.
Fungus fashion shows, oh what a sight,
Hats made of leaves, twinkling delight.

Roots are knitting beneath the street,
Swapping stories when the humans retreat.
A tickle attack from a branch above,
Nature's humor, it's hard not to love.

Shadows of the Canopy

Above me sways a leafy crowd,
Laughter erupts, oh my, how loud!
Squirrels juggling acorns in glee,
While birds quack jokes, quite merrily.

A sloth takes a nap, oh what a feat,
Dreaming of jellybeans, oh so sweet.
Vines swing like fashionistas on air,
Posing for cameras, without a care.

Each leaf flutters, a note in the wind,
Whispering punchlines that nature's pinned.
I try to catch them, but they play coy,
Hiding their giggles from this clumsy boy.

When shadows dance, I can't help but grin,
Tickling sunbeams, inviting me in.
Nature's comedy show, oh what a treat,
With laughter and legs on a tropical beat.

Roots in the Dark

Beneath the surface, roots have a ball,
Telling stories, they can't help but sprawl.
They tickle the toes of anyone near,
Sneaky little jests, spreading good cheer.

A meeting of mushrooms, so brightly dressed,
Challenging each other, who laughs the best?
Quips of the soil that nobody hears,
While gophers take bets on their peers.

Raccoons roll in, with masks on their face,
Declaring themselves the kings of this place.
They trip on the roots, it's a lovely sight,
Fumbling and tumbling, oh what a fright!

I chuckle softly, trying to peek,
At the rooty rascals that dance 'neath my feet.
In the dark they conspire, oh what a joke,
A secret comedy show, nature's cloak.

Secrets of the Underbrush

Under the leaves, they gather in rows,
Drawing up plans with quizzical prose.
Frogs run stand-up, making me laugh,
While snails take their time, no need to be fast.

A hedgehog consults with a fuzzy bee,
Discussing the latest in leaf fashion spree.
The toads play cards, betting on flies,
Throwing their chips with gleeful cries.

Crickets recite their nightly delights,
Making the moon giggle in delight.
While shadows sway, a dance so absurd,
Underneath all the jokes, not a soul heard.

A rabbit hops in, dropping one-liners,
Telling the tales of his grass-loving diners.
With jesters and jesting, all is well met,
In the underbrush where fun never lets.

The Murmurs of the Silent Earth

In the underbrush, a squabble ensues,
Frogs arguing fiercely about their best shoes.
A snail claims it's speed, but it's just in a hurry,
While ants hold a meeting, there's talk of a flurry.

Worms write in whispers, well hidden from view,
Sharing the news of the latest dew.
And here comes a beetle, strutting with pride,
With dreams of a crown, he's got nothing to hide.

Roots groove and wiggle, they dance underground,
While critters beneath giggle, in laughter profound.
They know all the secrets that the big world can miss,
In the mischief of soil, who wouldn't want bliss?

Every rustle and tumble tells stories untold,
Where the tiny and silly, their antics unfold.
So give a good listen, to the earth's funny chatter,
To those murmurs and whispers, it really does matter.

An Odyssey of Tiny Wonders

A tiny explorer sets out on a quest,
To find the best acorn, he knows it's the best.
He asks a wise squirrel, but she snickers and rolls,
'Last time you did that, you lost all your goals!'

The mushrooms are bright, like a candy parade,
Each one has a secret, a silly charade.
A ladybug giggles, as it flutters around,
Daring the grasshopper to make a big sound.

Each beetle has humor, a joke or a pun,
While crickets compose, thinking of ways to run.
They laugh through the shadows where the wild things hide,
In this tiny kingdom, there's no room for pride.

So the adventurer chuckles, a grin ear to ear,
With every discovery, he grows more sincere.
In this silly small world, the fun never ends,
With antics of laughter, and the joy of new friends.

Landscapes of the Inner Wild

In the cozy nook, where the wild things grow,
A hedgehog in pajamas, ready for a show.
He juggles some pebbles, while crickets all cheer,
But really, with charm, it's just luck, don't you fear!

Mice build a fortress of old twigs and leaves,
Crafting a castle that no one believes.
They sip on some dew, like it's the finest of wine,
Sharing giggles and stories, it's a grand little time.

A gecko does cartwheels on rocks shiny bright,
Claiming he's king of the magical night.
While fireflies twinkle, taking dance in the air,
Adding sparkle and laughter, everywhere.

So come join the fun, where the wild spirits play,
With nutty adventures sprouting each day.
In the heart of this realm, joy hangs like sweet fruit,
In landscapes of laughter, who needs a suit?

Footfalls in the Secret Green

Pitter-patter, it's a parade on the ground,
A troupe of small critters, with laughter abound.
The ants all conspire with plans for a feast,
While a butterfly flirts, oh what a wild beast!

A squirrel flips backward, almost like a pro,
While a rabbit takes notes, trying out the show.
They dance through the daisies, with hops and with rolls,
In their bustling community, they share all their goals.

Each step that they take, leaves a tale to unfold,
Of giggles and whispers, in the stories retold.
Their footprints are secrets, written in bliss,
In the sweet, blooming green, they'd never miss this!

So listen for footfalls, that tickle the ground,
Where fun is the language that's always around.
In the great secret green, where the tiny feet prance,
There's enough joy and laughter to make your heart dance!

Heartbeats of the Wilderness

In the thicket, I trip and I fall,
Owls hoot loudly, giving it their all.
A squirrel runs by, with nuts in tow,
I wave at a leaf, thinking it's a show.

Vines twist like dancers on jungle's floor,
Trying to escape, but they want to explore.
A parrot squawks jokes, who knew they'd be fine?
I laugh at my shoes, they're still wrapped in twine.

A frog leaps by, with a croak so loud,
Shooting for fame, he's dressed like a proud.
I join a parade with a beetle brigade,
Stomping and laughing, a ridiculous charade.

Roots tickle my toes, oh what a prank!
The ground giggles softly, it's got quite the prank.
Nature's a clown, don't you dare take a seat,
In this whimsical world, every laugh is a treat.

The Dance of Hidden Life

Underfoot marches a tiny brigade,
A worm in a top hat, so finely displayed.
Ants do a tango, a real showcase,
While beetles groove, at this thriving place.

Grass blades sway, in their zany trance,
Every step I take, makes them prance.
Watch out for the roots, they sneak on the side,
Wanting a tango, in nature they'll glide.

A caterpillar struts, like it owns the scene,
Making it known that it's the real queen.
In this dance hall, laughter spills with glee,
With figurative partners, do join the spree!

The ground is alive, a show so absurd,
Every critter chirps, no word is unheard.
With feet like maracas, I jump with delight,
Ignored by the earth, I dance out of sight.

Echoes from the Soil

Beneath my sole, whispers thread and weave,
Roots gossip loudly, you won't believe.
A drama unfolds, like a soap opera show,
The mushrooms argue, "Who's more in the know?"

A gopher peeks out, with eyes all askew,
"Is this the right place? I'm confused, who are you?"
The earthworms chuckle, as they wiggle around,
Sharing secrets from the deep underground.

A snail pulls a face, all slimy and bold,
Says, "I'm glamorous, or so I'm told!"
But I just keep laughing, at this underground chat,
It seems like I stepped on a comedy mat!

Echoes abound, in the grave and the cheer,
Nature's ensemble plays on, oh dear!
So I tiptoe softly, to keep their delight,
In a world full of jokes, where laughter takes flight.

Serenity Amongst the Vines

Vines embrace me like a giant hug,
Snakes wear shades—they think they're a thug!
The lizards lounge, sipping dew from a leaf,
While critters below play a game of belief.

A swing in the breeze, I'm caught in a spin,
The vines start to giggle, they know they can win.
With branches unfurling, they welcome my cheer,
It's a party of laughter, bring everyone here!

A spider spins tales, with silk like a rope,
"Have you heard the one about the hopin' ant's hope?"
I can't help but chuckle, they're all such a crew,
With vines as my blanket, I just can't be blue.

Serenity reigns, as the lanterns ignite,
Wildlife is grooving, oh what a sight!
In this carefree haven, the day starts to close,
With vines all around, I'm struck by their prose.

An Odyssey Through Plant-Laden Paths

As I stumble on roots, who knew they could trip?
The trees giggle softly, their branches all flip.
A snail wearing glasses, quite the sight to behold,
Invites me to tea, as secrets unfold.

With vines playing games, they swing all around,
I swear I heard laughter, from leaves on the ground.
A frog croaks a joke, quite punny and neat,
While ants join the party, on tiny, quick feet.

Beneath tangled ferns, the secrets they keep,
Are whispered by critters who never do sleep.
A raccoon tells tales of the berries he's found,
As I laugh at his antics, all lost in this round.

So indulge in the fun, let your worries take flight,
In paths full of flora, where day turns to night.
Nature's a stage, with a comedy flair,
So dance with your shadows, let out a wild cheer!

Harvesting Wishes from the Soil

Digging deep in the muck, oh what will I find?
A gnome with a shovel, he's quick and quite kind.
He offers me wishes, but check the fine print,
One week's worth of chuckles for a mighty short squint.

With cucumbers chatting, the peas start to roll,
I'm laughing so hard, they're taking a toll.
A tomato with swagger claims he's King of the Patch,
While radishes gossip, they seem quite attached.

Each seed is a wish, thrown into the dirt,
I pluck up the weeds that give me a spurt.
"Oh dear!" says a carrot, "I'm losing my top!"
But we giggle together, forgetting to stop.

So next time you dig, just join in the fun,
Harvesting laughter in the warm, loving sun.
A patch of pure joy, grown fresh from the ground,
With wishes and whims where delights can be found!

The Dance of Insects Beneath the Skies

The ants hold a dance, with a boogie so fine,
While weevils spin tales, sipping dew from a vine.
A cricket on beats, he leads with a cheer,
Says, "Join in the jig, let go of your fear!"

A beetle with flair showcases his moves,
He twirls like a ballerina, in polished grooves.
Fireflies flicker, they're the lights of the show,
As they sparkle and shimmer, putting on quite the glow.

With music from nature, it's a lively affair,
The buzzing and chirping, fills up the air.
"Who brought the snacks?" asks a curious fly,
"I've got fruit from the garden," shouts out a shy pie.

So hop, skip, and jump beneath that great moon,
For a gala of bugs, it happens too soon.
Join in the whirling, let your spirit ignite,
In this dance of the critters, till morning brings light!

Where Moss Holds Secrets

Underfoot is a carpet, soft as a dream,
Where rumors spin wild, or so it would seem.
A toad with a grin, claims gossip for days,
As the moss giggles softly, in cryptic displays.

With cushions of green, they invite me to sit,
A chat with the mushrooms, who won't let me quit.
They whisper of things from the roots to the sky,
And I can't help but laugh, as we all give a try.

"Who hides in the shadows?" a squirrel starts to muse,
With acorns like jewels, he's banking on clues.
Each lichen holds tales of the rain and the sun,
As I listen intently, this gathering's fun.

So when you walk softly, take heed of the ground,
For secrets of moss might just blur all around.
Embrace these weird whispers, let your heart skip a beat,
In the world made of laughter, oh, how sweet!

www.ingramcontent.com/pod-product-compliance
Lightning Source LLC
Chambersburg PA
CBHW070321120526
44590CB00017B/2770